Your friend, John

50 creative sparks
TO ENCOURAGE
writing

BY JOHN JACOBSON

The original purchaser of this book and enhanced CD has permission to reproduce the student letters and journal activities for educational use in one school only. Any other use is strictly prohibited. This material is not for broadcast or transmission of any kind, and is not for resale.

HAL•LEONARD®
CORPORATION
7777 W. BLUEMOUND RD. P.O. BOX 13819 MILWAUKEE, WI 53213

Visit Hal Leonard Online at
www.halleonard.com

T0055789

Table of Contents

I. Citizenship

II. Music

III. Holidays & Happenings

Dear Readers,

Welcome to "Your friend, John!"

John, that's me. I hope that through this year we get to know each other better and better. After all, reading and writing together is a great way to make friends and learn all kinds of new things.

Personally, I spend most of my time in music class. Some of the most important things I ever learned, I learned in there. I learned about history, about languages, even about math and social studies. In music class I also learned that I mattered. That's right! Sometimes the world can seem so big and filled with so many people that it's easy to forget that each person in that world is important. In music class I learned that it takes all kinds of people, with all different interests and talents to make a world filled with harmony.

Everyone is important, including you!

In this book, I've written you fifty letters. They are just thoughts I had that I hoped you wouldn't mind reading and thinking about.

Your thoughts are important, too.

So, I was thinking that it would be great for you to have a place to write down your own thoughts just like I did in this book. I hope you will use this as a place to "express" yourself. After each one of my letters to you, I will provide a "starter" question, phrase or suggestion and you take it from there. Anything you feel, express it!

Writing needs to be practiced just like making music. You will probably get to be a better writer the more you do it. Besides that, sometimes it helps you sort out your own thoughts and ideas when you write them down. If you decide to share them with your teacher, parents and friends, even better! Sharing ideas with your friends ... what could be better than that?

Come on, let's get started.

ENHANCED CD

Your friend, John

50 creative sparks TO ENCOURAGE writing

50 MP3 audio recordings of John's letters

PDFs of 50 Letters & Creative Writing Sheets

COMPACT disc+ DIGITAL AUDIO

MP3 AUDIO

This disc contains MP3 files and is intended for MP3-CD players and computers.

HAL•LEONARD®

About the Enhanced MP3 CD

The enclosed CD is a **data disc** containing **mp3 files** of John's recorded letters and **PDFs** of the letters and journal writing activities. This disc may be used with computers, mp3 compatible CD players and car stereos. If imported into your computer, you can access the tracks with any mp3 player, such as an iPod.

➡ **50 MP3 audio recordings of John reading the letters for a personal touch**

➡ **50 letters to print or project**

➡ **50 journal activity sheets for creative writing**

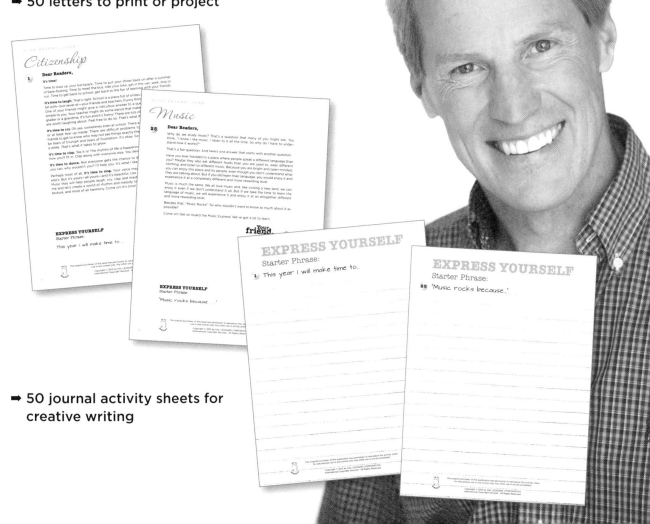

Citizenship

Dear Readers,

It's time!

Time to load up your backpack. Time to put your shoes back on after a summer of bare-footing. Time to meet the bus, ride your bike, get in the van, walk, skip or run. Time to get back to school; get back to the fun of learning with your friends.

It's time to laugh. That's right. School is a place full of smiles and laughter, laughter with—but never at—your friends and teachers. Funny things happen at school. One of your friends might give a ridiculous answer to a question that seems so simple to you. Your teacher might do some dance that makes her look like a third grader or a grandma. It's fun and it's funny! There are lots of things in school that are worth laughing about. Feel free to do so. That's what it takes to grow.

It's time to cry. Oh yes, sometimes even at school. There are things to cry about, or at least tear up inside. There are difficult problems to solve. There are new friends to get to know who may not see things exactly the way you do. There will be tears of triumph and tears of frustration. It's okay. Go ahead and cry once in a while. That's what it takes to grow.

It's time to clap. Yes it is! The rhythm of life is happening and you get to decide how you'll fit in. Clap along with everyone else. You deserve a little applause.

It's time to dance. Not everyone gets the chance to dance, but you do. And if you can, why wouldn't you? I'll help you. It's what I like to do.

Perhaps most of all, **it's time to sing.** Your voice may not sound like everyone else's. But it's yours—all yours—and it's beautiful. Use your voice to make music. Music that will help people laugh, cry, clap and maybe even dance. Come with me and let's create a world of rhythm and melody, tempo and tone, timbre and texture, and most of all harmony. Come on! It's time!

EXPRESS YOURSELF
Starter Phrase:

This year I will make time to ...

2

Dear Readers,

"Be nice!" Did anybody ever say that to you? Maybe it was your mom or dad, grandmother or grandfather. Maybe it was your teacher. Maybe it was a friend.

"Be nice." It is only two words, but I think that it is pretty good advice, don't you?

There's another saying that people sometimes say, but I personally do not believe. It says that, "Nice guys finish last," but you know what? In my long life, I have NEVER found that to be true. My experience has taught me that nice guys are always the winners. And when I say "guys," I mean "girls," too. Nice guys and nice girls always win. It just depends on how you define "winning."

Being nice is not always easy. Sometimes there will be someone who comes into your life that just rubs you the wrong way. Maybe they make you feel jealous, hurt or angry. Maybe they look, dress or act differently than you and your friends, so it is easy to make a joke about them, or talk about them behind their back. Maybe they get to do something you don't get to do, like sing a solo in the spring concert or play the quarterback while you end up at center. Maybe you think that they get all the breaks. Maybe they just haven't been very nice to you so you think, "Why should I be nice to them?"

Here is why. **Nice people win.** You still might not get to sing the solo and you still might have to hike the ball instead of pass it, but believe me, you win. I have met a lot of people in my life, from Presidents and Prime Ministers to sports idols and movie stars and I can tell you honestly that the greatest were also the nicest. They treated people with respect. They gave everybody even more than a second chance. They were kind. They were nice. That is what made them winners.

I have a challenge for all of you that I hope you will take very seriously.

Be nice.

- If there is someone getting on your nerves or bothering you, **be nice.**
- If you are feeling jealous because someone got something you didn't, **be nice.**
- If you see someone who is different and you think that making a joke about them to your friends would be fun, **be nice.**

Be nice, and you will be a winner every time.

Your friend, John

EXPRESS YOURSELF
Starter Phrase:

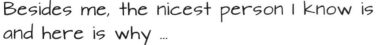
Besides me, the nicest person I know is _____, and here is why ...

3

Dear Readers,

What do you think it means when you sing or say to someone, "You raise me up?" Do you think it means that they actually have to lift you off the ground? No, probably not. It might be funny to say to an elevator operator, "Hey! You raise me up!" But it's hard to find an elevator operator these days, even for a good joke. I suppose you could say, "You raise me up!" to an airline pilot. After all, they are the ones who get us off the ground with the help of propellers or a jet and a couple of wings. But, I don't think that is actually the meaning of the phrase "you raise me up" in its best sense either.

I think that we all have people in our lives to whom we could say, "You raise me up." It's a person who helps you discover your best qualities. It's a person who helps you to do better in life, or like they say in the Olympics, go "faster, higher, stronger." For some of us, it might be a parent, a brother or sister, an aunt or uncle, or a grandmother or grandfather. Maybe it's one or more of your teachers, or someone in the community that you know and who really knows you. Maybe it's a good friend that you have had for a long time and is always there when you need them.

Maybe you are lucky and have many people in your life that "raise you up." I guarantee that every single one of you has someone in your life that would like to. They are a person who cares about you and will never give up on you, no matter what. They will make you grow. They will make you strong. They will make you better, if you let them.

Can you think of anybody that "raises you up?" If not, then stop reading. Look up to the front of the room. Do you see that teacher standing there? There is at least one person who will help you stand on mountains, walk on stormy seas and be more than you ever thought you could be. Let them. It will be a wonderful ride.

Your friend,
John

EXPRESS YOURSELF
Starter Phrase:

One person who raises me up is _____.
And here is how . . .

4

Dear Readers,

What could be better than spending your days searching for love, hope, charity, harmony, friendship and truth – all leading to a world where everybody lives in peace?

I have a dog. His name is Shadow. He is half German Shepherd and half wolf, which makes him very smart and very hungry! Even though he's all white, I named him Shadow for two reasons: One, we live on Shadow Valley Ranch, and two, I love that movie *Homeward Bound*. I especially love the part when the old dog Shadow comes running over the hill and the little boy yells "Shadow!" as they run toward each other for a tearful reunion. (Well, at least I'm always tearful when I watch that scene.) My Shadow is an extremely friendly dog and loves everybody, especially the UPS man, who wisely has a treat for him in his right coat pocket when he makes a delivery to the ranch.

What about you? Do you have a pet, too? Maybe you have a dog or a cat, a hamster or a rabbit, a fish or a ferret to keep you company. It's amazing how sometimes our pets know just what we're thinking or feeling. In return, we can usually tell what they are thinking as well. Shadow seems to know just when I need a slobbery lick on the cheek, or to go for a run. He also knows how much I like it when he lies by my feet when I'm working at my desk.

Shadow and I have a lot of adventures together on Shadow Valley Ranch. Shadow thinks that a quest for peace is a noble activity for every man or beast. He also thinks that a quest pursued together with friends is the best quest to be on. Because, when we work together, we can do amazing things. I agree. Don't you?

Your friend,
John

P.S. Shadow says "Arf, arf, bow wow!" which means "Your friend, Shadow," but you probably already knew that.

EXPRESS YOURSELF
Starter Phrase:

Write about an adventure you have had with your pet or your imaginary pet.

OK TO REPRODUCE

Dear Readers,

Do you sometimes find yourself doing something or saying something, and inside your head you're thinking, "Wait a minute! That's not me! Why am I doing this? Why am I saying this?"

Why do you think this happens? Maybe it's because of peer pressure. Maybe we think we have to do this or say this because it's the cool thing to do or say. Maybe all your friends are doing it and saying it, so you think you'd better too, or you might not fit in.

For instance, one time I heard a boy talking to another boy. He said, "You know, I don't really like music class. It's not my thing." The second boy hesitated and then muttered, "Yeah, I know what you mean. I don't like it either."

Well, I was shocked! The reason I was shocked is that I know this second boy very well. I happen to know for a fact that he really LOVES music class. It definitely is "his thing." I think he said what he said because he didn't want to be different. He wanted to think and act just like his friend.

It isn't always easy just being you, honest to goodness, plain old you. But you know what? Plain old you is pretty special. You are the only one in the whole universe with your exact hair color, size, voice quality, sense of humor, brainpower and more. You are the only one that thinks your exact thoughts, feels your exact feelings, smells your exact smell. You are you, the one and only.

It's the start of a brand new year. Let's you and I decide that with the start of this year, we're going to celebrate all that it is to be ourselves. Let's encourage others to be themselves, too. We don't have to agree on everything or like the same things, but let's respect each other as we all figure out what "bein' me" is all about.

You're you. I'm me. Plain old, exceptional, one-of-a kind you and me! How cool is that?

Your friend, John

EXPRESS YOURSELF
Starter Phrase:

Write about this thought –
This is what it means to be me.

6

Dear Readers,

Do you ever feel nervous about trying something new? You want to jump in, but you are afraid you won't be any good at it. People might laugh at you. You might fail. I want to encourage you to give it your very best effort. Who knows? There may be parts of this new adventure that you really love. You'll never know unless you give it a try.

"Jumping" reminds me of a story that I heard not too long ago. I think it's a good one.

This story is about a group of little green frogs that decided to have a contest to see who could hop their way to the very top of a tall tower. There were dozens of frogs and the tower was indeed very tall. When the day of the race came, a lot of their friends – ducks, cows, chickens and even some teachers – showed up to see what was going to happen. After all, who doesn't like to see a green frog hopping up a tower? Nobody really thought the frogs would get to the top. It was so very high. Never the less, the duck quacked and the little green frogs started hopping.

"You'll never make it!" some of the spectators cried. "Give up now!" "You haven't got a chance!" It wasn't long before some of the frogs did drop out. "You're making fools of yourselves!" the chicken hollered. "It's too high! It's impossible!" the cow mooed. The frogs kept jumping, but more and more dropped out. "No frog is ever going to make it to the top of that tower!" burped a toad. Eventually, all of the frogs did drop out. All that is, except one, who made it to the very top. Do you know why that frog made it to the top of the tower? That one frog was totally deaf.

You see, he couldn't hear all of the spectators telling him that he couldn't do something that he had his heart set on. He just kept jumping until he reached the top, turned round and waved to the crowd below.

If you're feeling a little nervous about trying something new, I hope that you will be like that little green frog and jump in with your whole heart. Don't listen to any voices that tell you "you can't do it." I know you can! So do a lot of other toads, cows, chickens and teachers. Come on! Jump in!

Your friend,
John

EXPRESS YOURSELF
Starter Phrase:

Write about what it was like to try something for the first time.

Dear Readers,

Have you ever gone for a walk down a road or a path and you had no idea where you were going? It can be very exciting and maybe even a little frightening at times. Who knows what's around that next corner? It might be a beautiful meadow or a busy city. It might be full of people, or you might find yourself walking all alone.

Starting a new school year can be like that. You show up to your school. You see some old friends and some people you hardly know at all. You might have a new teacher, or many new teachers. You see books and computers full of new information. You kind of know what is going to happen. You are going to study reading and math, history and science, art, physical fitness and so many more things, but there is lot you don't know as well.

Still, you are very brave. You show up, follow the rules, start down that road and let the learning begin.

Making music is an especially exciting road to be traveling on. You start with beat, then add a little melody, maybe some harmony and soon, you're making music. This road can be full of fantastic surprises. There will be lots of new songs. You might learn to play the recorder or some percussion instruments. You might study great composers, make up some dances, or even put on a show. One thing for sure, the musical path you walk down will never be boring.

Children all over the world are walking on the same musical road you are on. Keep your eyes and ears open. It's a road full of amazing surprises! And I'll be right beside you all the way!

EXPRESS YOURSELF
Starter Phrase:

Here's the starter phrase for your own story.
"One day I was walking down a road I had never been on before. I turned a corner and here is what happened."

8

Dear Readers,

What does freedom mean to you? Franklin Delano Roosevelt, the 32nd President of the United States, said that there were four freedoms that everybody in the world deserves.

- The first is freedom of speech and expression...everywhere in the world.
- The second is the freedom of every person to worship God in his own way... everywhere in the world.
- The third is freedom from want...everywhere in the world.
- The fourth is freedom from fear...anywhere in the world.

In America, we assume that we can voice our opinion and not be punished for it. That doesn't mean you can say or sing whatever you want whenever you want, because with freedom comes, responsibility. Some of those responsibilities include respecting other people's feelings and opinions, too.

In America, we assume that we can worship God in our own way, but that doesn't mean that we can do whatever we want, because with freedom comes responsibility. Some of those responsibilities include respecting other people's feelings, opinions and beliefs.

In America, we assume that we will all not want. That means that we think we will have enough to eat, a decent place to live, a good education, a doctor when we need one and good clothes upon our back, but with those necessities comes responsibility. Some of those responsibilities include paying taxes to support schools, hospitals and organizations that help people who may not be free from want.

In America, we assume that we will be free from fear. We feel like we will be protected, but with that freedom comes responsibilities. Some of those responsibilities include trying to understand our neighbors' wants and fears, and helping them to live free of fear, too. It means sharing the bounty of freedom, like our president said... "everywhere in the world."

In every case, what word seems to fit right next to the word freedom? If you guessed "responsibility," you are absolutely right, because freedom isn't free, but it is worth the price.

Your friend,
John

EXPRESS YOURSELF
Starter Phrase:

What does freedom mean to you?

9

Dear Readers,

There is always a time for dreams. There is always a place for dreamers.

Every single person that has ever walked, run, hunted, hid or slept has had dreams that they were following.

Remember the pilgrims of the first Thanksgiving? They dreamed of a land where they could live in peace and worship as they please.

Do you remember the King Massasoit? He dreamed of lands where he and his people could hunt and live in peace, close to nature.

A little girl who fell asleep under the tree in mid-December? She dreamed too, of warmth, of home.

The slaves who followed the signs of the Freedom Train had dreams. They dreamed of freedom. They dreamed that "someday their little children would live in a country where they would be judged not by the color of their skin, but by the content of their character." Martin Luther King, Junior said that. He was a dreamer, too.

Abraham Lincoln was a dreamer. He dreamed of a land united, where all would live free.

Now, I'm looking at you. I am telling you that I believe in you. I am telling you to take time to dream, because I have seen it over and over again, that it is the dreamers like you who will make the world a better place to grow.

Keep dreaming, readers and writers. Keep dreaming.

We believe in you.

EXPRESS YOURSELF
Starter Phrase:

"I have a dream that..."

10

Dear Readers,

Spring is a time for planters.

Did I ever tell you about my brother Steve? He's quite a guy. First of all, he's very smart. He's a fine debater. He teaches high school history and Social Studies, so I think you get to be a pretty good debater doing that. He helps his students become good debaters, too, just like Abraham Lincoln and Stephen A. Douglas. He's a coach of all kinds of sports. He's a wonderful uncle to his nieces and nephews, good to his mother and good to his little brother, too. (That would include me and a few others.) But most of all, I think of Steve as a planter. Yep! That's right. Well, "what does he plant?" you might ask and have every right to do so. My answer is, "He plants peace." That's right, **peace**.

You see, a few years ago my brother's town built a brand new high school right in the middle of town. It is beautiful. However, out in the front of the school was a huge, flat lawn that had not been given much consideration when the school was built. My brother thought, "You know, just like a gift, a new building is always much more appreciated if it is wrapped in something beautiful." So my smart, coaching, debating, planter brother Steve decided that he would make it into a garden: not just any garden, mind you, but a Peace Garden. He dug it all up and started planting beautiful flowers and trees. Students and teachers and lots of friends started seeing how nice it was to plant a Peace Garden and they joined in the effort. They put in sprinklers to water the plants, built a little amphitheater so that classes could meet outside and talk about peace, and placed marble benches throughout the garden engraved with quotes by brilliant people from all over the world encouraging peace on earth, good will toward men. Now, whenever anybody goes to the garden, they read about, think about and talk about **peace**. Everybody in town eventually goes there and so everybody eventually starts talking about peace.

Now, my sister Sherry has started a Peace Garden at the elementary school where she teaches sixth grade and I'm starting one at my house. Do you see what I mean about Steve being a planter? He planted tress, flowers and good ideas. Eventually, everybody's going to be talking about **peace**. How about you joining the conversation, too?

Thanks, Steve, and all of the other peace planters in the world.

EXPRESS YOURSELF
Starter Phrase:

Write a poem about peace.

Dear Readers,

I think that there is no more perfect song about our country than the song "America, the Beautiful." The words were written by an English teacher by the name of Katherine Lee Bates just after she had been on top of Pike's Peak in Colorado. The music is by a man named Samuel Ward. He wrote it while on a boat in New York Harbor just about exactly where our Statue of Liberty now stands. I think I'll go out on a limb and say that it is one of my favorite songs of all time. To me, it is a perfect example of when just the right poetry meets just the right melody to make just the right song.

I love it all, but my favorite verse is the one that says:

> *O beautiful for patriot dream*
> *That sees beyond the years,*
> *Thine alabaster cities gleam*
> *Undimmed by human tears.*

I think what Katherine Bates was trying to say here is that while it's true that America is beautiful for its purple mountain majesties and amber waves of grain, what really makes America a great nation is the vision that our ancestors had for it. It was their vision that our country would be a land that was "great" but also "good." Ms. Bates reminds us that we need to crown our greatness with goodness and our bounty with brotherhood. If we do that, that noble vision of our founding mothers and fathers will never be dimmed by human tears.

That's what makes America, the Beautiful.

Your friend,
John

EXPRESS YOURSELF
Starter Phrase:

Write a new verse for the song "America, the Beautiful."

12

Dear Readers,

Did you ever hear the story of "The Little Engine That Could?" It has always been one of my favorites. It's about a very small locomotive engine that helps pull a trainload of toys over the mountain to the waiting children on the other side. She's a very small engine and it's a very big mountain. Nobody watching would ever believe that this little engine could possibly accomplish such an amazing feat. But the little engine is so determined not to let the children down, that she gives it her very best, chugging along and chanting, "I think I can! I think I can! I think I can!" She believes in herself, and guess what? She makes it!

Did you ever try something that everybody who knows you thought you could never do . . . like riding a skateboard for the very first time, playing a musical instrument or spelling hippopotamus? Just wanting to do something doesn't always make it possible. You might actually have to practice riding a skateboard before you get very good at it, or you might actually have to study before you can spell hippopotamus. Imagine that! But if you don't believe in yourself, it can be hard to do almost anything, especially something as hard as riding a skate-board, playing a musical instrument, spelling hippopotamus or pulling a train full of toys over a gigantic mountain.

Next time something very challenging is put in front of you, I hope that you will remember the story of "The Little Engine That Could" and repeat right out loud, or in your head, "I think I can! I think I can! I think I can!" Next, work very hard to attain that goal by practicing, studying or doing whatever is necessary to pre-pare yourself for the task you believe in your heart you can do.

Then, when the challenge is there, you can proudly be the one to step forward and confidently say, "Yes, I can! Yes, I can! Yes, I can!"

I believe in you.

P.S. By the way, it's H-I-P-P-O-P-O-T-A-M-U-S!
I looked it up!

EXPRESS YOURSELF
Starter Phrase:

"This year, I think I can . . ."

13

Dear Readers,

From May 25 to September 17 way back in 1787, a group of American men got together in Philadelphia and drafted what was soon to be the Constitution of the United States of America. It might have happened a lot quicker had a few women been included, but never-the-less, the amazing document that these patriots wrote is the very foundation this country stands upon.

It begins with what we call a Preamble, or an introduction: "We the People of the United States in order to form a more perfect Union . . . " Wow! What a start!

To me, the Preamble to our constitution is why America is a great country. In 1787, there had never really been a land where people from all over the world had come together and had decided to live and to work side by side as equals. More than two hundred and thirty years later, it continues to be something very special.

When our forefathers wrote those words — "We the People"— they said a mouthful. They said that in this country, we would all do our best to make sure that every person will have an equal voice and equal opportunity. There will be people who look different, speak differently, worship differently, sing, dress and dance differently than their neighbors. In this new country, those differences will be a cause for celebration. For here is a nation where it is no longer just about me or just about you. It is about "We the People."

It takes a lot of courage to live, work and even sing next to people who might seem very different from you. Sometimes we may not even agree with the sound they are making, the words they are singing or the dance they are dancing. But you know what? The more we listen and try to understand the people around us, the more "perfect" our union might become.

Yes, it takes courage to believe in "We the People," but that, my friends, is also why America is "the land of the free and the home of the (you said it) brave."

That's why I love America and I hope you do, too.

Your friend,
John

EXPRESS YOURSELF
Starter Phrase:

"I can be a positive citizen of the United States by . . ."

Dear Readers,

I've been watching a lot of basketball lately. It's a great sport and the players we see on television are amazing athletes. It's astounding how they seem to fly through the air, how fast they can get up and down the court, how they can shoot three-pointers hitting nothing but net. Some of these basketball players have become very famous and very wealthy because of their amazing abilities on the court.

All that fame and fortune must be pretty exciting.

But today I am reminded of something that one of the greatest basketball players of all time once said. He played for the NBA Champion Detroit Pistons back in the '80s and '90s. He was very famous for being a fantastic basketball player. But do you know what he said? He said, "If all I'm remembered for is being a good basketball player, then I've done a bad job with the rest of my life."

What do you suppose he meant by that?

Here's what I think he meant. We are all lots of things. We are brothers and sisters, cousins, sons and daughters. We are students, athletes, writers, readers, singers, dancers and so much more. We are friends.

Which do you think is more important to that famous athlete – to be a good basketball player or to be a good son? To be a good basketball player or to be a good student? To be a great basketball player or to be a great friend? I think we all know what he would say.

How about you? What do you say?

EXPRESS YOURSELF
Starter Phrase:

"I can be a great friend by . . ."

Dear Readers,

I love to travel! It's been a lot of fun for me remembering adventures I've had in different places around the world, telling you about them and even writing a song to match.

I've been very lucky to do a lot of traveling in my life—sometimes for work, but often just for the adventure of it. I think traveling is such an important part of life. It helps you grow and to learn about and understand people and places that are different than you.

Somebody once said, "Life is a book." Someone followed that up by saying, "If life is a book and you never travel, then you have only read the first page!"

Traveling isn't always easy. In fact, it is often tempting just to stay home. But every time you go someplace new, you write a new page in the book that is your life. I think that is worth the hassle.

Since most of you are still in school, you probably don't have too much time to travel. I know that constantly studying, practicing your music, and doing nice things for your teacher takes a lot of time. But when you get a little older, I hope that you will grab any opportunity to travel and see as much of the world as you possibly can. I hope that you will try all kinds of different foods, hear all kinds of languages and dance to all kinds of music. I hope that the book that is your life is thick with pages full of adventures – adventures that you discovered as you explored this rocking, musical planet.

Your friend, John

EXPRESS YOURSELF
Starter Phrase:

Someday, I would like to travel to . . .

Dear Readers,

16

Welcome to a brand new year! Welcome to a year full of renewed hope and unlimited possibility.

One of the best things about beginning a new year is that we all can feel like this year we're going to get it right. Not that we didn't do well last year, but there is always room for improvement, right?

What do you think I mean when I say get "it" right?

"It" might mean different things to different people. But in our country there are certain "its" that we all agree upon. We agree that we want to live in a land of freedom and respect for the individual. We also agree that all men and women are created equal and that we all have certain rights that cannot be denied. We believe in "life, liberty and the pursuit of happiness." That's what people like George Washington, Abraham Lincoln and Martin Luther King, Jr. lived and sometimes died for. They believed in "it." We all believe in "it."

For more than 200 years, people in America have started each year with a sincere song of freedom and liberty in their hearts. Each New Year, we wake up hoping, believing and promising that this year we will work hard to keep that song of America alive and sing it ever more in tune. When we all put our hearts and hopes together, we know that this year we can get "it" ever more right. Right?

Like the song says, "This can be, everybody. This can be!"

Your friend,
John

EXPRESS YOURSELF
Starter Phrase:

This year is full of possibilities! I can . . .

Dear Readers,

I once wrote a song called "Any Kid Could Be President." Now, you are probably thinking, "So?"

Well, to me, the idea that any kid could be president is interesting because here in America we live with a form of government called a democracy. That means that everybody has a voice in deciding how our country is going to be run. One of the things we decide on is who will be our president. I realize that none of you are running yet, but one day you could, because you live in a country where every adult citizen has the right to vote and to run for office.

Do you know where most of the ideas about democracy came from? If you guessed Greece, you are absolutely right. In fact, the word democracy comes from the words in Greek that mean "rule of the people." So not only did Greece come up with the idea for the Olympics, but they also came up with the form of government that we use in our country today — not to mention baklava and some great circle dances!

We celebrate America as we elect the people who will lead our country. We also celebrate Greece and the gift they gave us in the form of democracy. Finally, we celebrate that we live in a country in which every child, including you, might grow up to be the next president of the United States!

To me, that's something to sing about.

Your friend, John

EXPRESS YOURSELF
Starter Phrase:

If I were president, I would . . .

18

Dear Readers,

I once wrote a song called "Superstar!" It is about being true to oneself. It is about having dreams and going after them. It is about believing that every one of us can be a superstar in his or her very own way.

What does it mean to you to be a superstar?

This morning, I read an article in the newspaper about a young girl who I think is a real superstar. Her name is Vanessa, and she is nine years old. She goes to a school in a rough part of town. At her school, they have decided to make the school day longer. They offer lots of activities after school. Some students take dance lessons, others play sports and games on the playground, and some take time to do their homework for the next day.

I think this is a good idea, because it gives the students a safe place to be until their parents come home from work. They also get to be with their friends and teachers that much longer. Vanessa is one of those students who is used to riding the bus home late and actually loves staying after school. In the newspaper article, Vanessa says, "I like sharing and being helpful. Sometimes when other kids try to do their homework and don't know the answer, I say, 'I'll help you.'"

Helping other people is one way that you can be a star.

Vanessa is a superstar to me. Thank you, Vanessa. And thanks to all of you readers who look around for someone who needs you and say, "I'll help you."

You are all Superstars!

Your friend,
John

EXPRESS YOURSELF
Starter Phrase:

"I can be a superstar by . . . "

19

Dear Readers,

I have some questions for you. After I ask these questions, there will be a one-word answer that works for every one of them. Here are my questions.

Is a pledge the same as a promise?

When you say "I pledge allegiance to the flag of the United States of America..." are you making a promise to your country that you will be loyal? The flag is a symbol of that country and all that it is and stands for. Is that country the beautiful land we live in, with "spacious skies and amber waves of grain"? Is it "purple mountains majesties, above the fruited plain"?

But is it more? When you say "I pledge allegiance to the flag of the United States of America..." are you making a promise to the people of our land? Are you promising that you will work and live along side them as one nation, unable to be divided, working for the common good of other Americans as well as your own good?

But is it more? When you say "I pledge allegiance to the flag of the United States of America..." are you promising that you are willing to stand up for your rights and the rights of others who also deserve to have that freedom and liberty?

And the answer to all of my questions is "_ _ _!"

I'm proud to be an American. Are you?

I hope you use the same answer as you used above.

EXPRESS YOURSELF
Starter Phrase:

Write your own version of The Pledge of Allegiance.

20

Dear Readers,

I have always loved the song "Stand By Me."

We all need people in our lives who will be there for us in good times or in bad. Can you think of someone in your life who stands by you no matter what? If you can't think of anybody right off the bat, perhaps you should just look to the front of the room at that teacher standing there. Your teachers are there because they believe in you. They believe that you are worth their time and energy and they want to help you be the very best that you can be. They expect a lot of you. Sometimes, you might think that they expect too much. But they expect a lot because they know you have a lot of potential in you, and you are capable of doing amazing things. They believe that someday you are going to be a successful adult, and they want to help you get there. That's why they are standing by you now and all year long.

In some ways, it's easier to be someone's friend when everything is going wrong for that friend. You can offer them your shoulder to cry on and be their hero. Often times, it is more difficult to be someone's friend when everything seems to be going right for them. It's easy to get envious and not want to be happy for their success. But a true friend stands by their friends in good times and in bad, in happy times and in sad. What kind of friend are you?

There's one more thing I wanted to say to you this month, and the song "Stand By Me" gives me a reason to say it. You are not alone. There are people everywhere who care about you and who are standing by you, believing that you are worth every ounce of effort. One of them is...

Your friend,
John

EXPRESS YOURSELF
Starter Phrase:

Write about an experience in which you stood by someone or someone stood by you.

Dear Readers,

It's Spring, or at least it's close to Spring in most parts of our continent! It's a time when gardeners place tiny seeds in the soil, nurture them with water and maybe a little fertilizer, and then let nature take its course. Almost always, something miraculous happens. The sun shines. The rain falls. From that little seed sprouts a shoot that grows into a mature plant. Then that plant grows a flower, then fruit and then seeds so the entire miracle starts all over again. It is truly something to celebrate. Let it grow! Celebrate the world!

You and I are not plants, but, like plants, we are a part of that circle of life. Also, like plants, we are something to celebrate.

When you are young, you are like that seed and that sprout. You are starting to grow into something that is uniquely you. Some of us will grow very tall. Others, not so much. One of the biggest differences between us and a plant is that we make choices along the way. Let's face it, when a bean seed starts to grow, it's going to grow to be a bean plant. When an acorn is planted, it is going to turn into an oak, if everything goes well. But unlike a bean or an acorn, you and I will to make choices all along the way as to the kind of being we want to be.

How will we know if the decisions we make are the best choices that will allow us to become all that we can be? We make these decisions by listening to our hearts and thinking with our heads. Listening to your heart and thinking with your head means you think about what it is you love and what it is that interests you. You learn as much as you can about those interests and try to do your best at what your head and heart are telling you to pursue. You always keep yourself open to new possibilities because, as you grow, your interests might change and so might the thoughts in your head and the feelings of your heart. That's called growing. It's nothing to be afraid of; it's something to celebrate.

Let it grow! Celebrate the world!

EXPRESS YOURSELF
Starter Phrase:

"I celebrate the world when I......"

22

Dear Readers,

I can see it! The end of the school year is almost here!

It's May, or June, depending on when you read this letter. For most of you that means it is getting close to the end of the school year and you are looking forward to a nice vacation! I hope you have exciting plans and that some of those plans involve music. Actually, I can hardly think of a meaningful summer activity that doesn't include music. Beach time, outdoor concerts, parades, festivals, summer camps, and even baseball games use music to make the summer atmosphere even more festive.

I also hope that as this school year comes to an end and you look forward to coming back in the fall in a new grade level, you take some time to think about all the people that helped you get to this moment in your life. After all, none of us can do it all by ourselves. It takes a lot of people's unselfish efforts to make sure we have the opportunity to learn, grow, try new things and be safe while we do so.

How many times have those important people in your life said something to you like this? "You are a special person with a special song to sing and I'm here to help you discover it," or "I'm here to help you be the best that you can be." They may not say it exactly like that, but I think you know what I mean. Your parents, grandparents, aunts and uncles, the school administration, the custodians and cooks, coaches and aides, office help and especially your teachers have been there for you all year long for one reason – to help you grow into the beautiful, intelligent, courageous, courteous, cooperative, honest, trustworthy and caring person you are. They saw it in you all along. I hope you can see it too.

So as the school year comes to a close, I want to encourage you to pause for a moment and think about all of the people in your life who are trying to help you on your journey to become the best that you can be; and before this year is over, I hope you will make an effort to say those two words they deserve to hear and which will mean the world to them – "thank you!"

They have helped make you the special person you are. I can see it.

Your friend,
John

EXPRESS YOURSELF
Starter Phrase:

Write about a person or persons who you can see has helped you make it through this year and is helping you be the best that you can be.

Dear Readers,

Have you ever thought to yourself, "I want to be just like that person," or even, "I wish I was that person?" Sometimes when you see somebody that you really admire, somebody who can do things that you find amazing, it's natural to want to be like them.

But this month, I have three little words to share with you. Those three words are "You are enough." You — the one and only — are enough.

You see, I love to watch Steve Nash play basketball and David Beckham play soccer. But we don't need another Steve Nash or David Beckham — not exactly. I love Lady Gaga. But we have a Lady Gaga, and as wonderful and creative as she is, we need new "wonderful and creative" — not a do-over.

You don't have to try to be somebody that you are not. This does not mean that you can do whatever you please. There are still rules and guidelines that we all embrace if we want to live in an orderly and civil society. Kindness, sympathy, generosity, honesty, courage, respect, and being fair are just some of the things we should all work on.

But you can do all of that and still be the unique individual that you are. You are okay. You are better than okay. You are miraculous. Just be the best that you can be. That will be enough. You — kind, trustworthy, respectful, caring, responsible and fair — you are enough.

EXPRESS YOURSELF
Starter Phrase:

I am unique because . . .

24

Dear Readers,

In America, we often talk about "The American Dream." What does that mean to you?

When the great men and women that founded our country more than two centuries ago declared our nation's independence from foreign countries, they stated that,

> "We hold these truths to be self evident that all men are created equal. That they are endowed by their Creator with certain inalienable rights. That among these are life, liberty and the pursuit of happiness."

Those are awesome words.

Maybe, the American Dream can best be summed up as trying to live up to those words. Maybe it means that we dream about a country where everybody IS treated equal; a country where everybody can expect to enjoy their "inalienable rights" of "life, liberty and the pursuit of happiness."

Most people probably agree, that we have come a long way as a free nation. In America, we enjoy more rights and freedoms than any place on earth. We can worship as we please. We can speak freely when we have an opinion. We can all seek happiness in our own special way. But most of us also agree that there is still work to be done to make sure that everybody gets their fair share of that American Dream.

In the autumn, we celebrate Veterans Day. It's a wonderful chance to show our appreciation for all of the men and women who have served our country in military service. I sometimes wonder what could keep a soldier going when he or she is far from home, far away from the people they love. I wonder how they kept working in the muddy trenches, arid deserts, steamy jungles, stormy seas or dangerous airs of war. If you ask them, they might all have a very different answer.

But I think the most common answer you would get from those American heroes is that they kept on working because they believed in – that's right – the American Dream! I also think, that they kept going because they wanted to make sure that the loved ones that they left behind and the loved ones that followed, like you and me, could live that American Dream in peace. I hope that we never forget what they gave so that we could pursue our dreams!

Your friend,
John

EXPRESS YOURSELF
Starter Phrase:

"To me the American Dream means . . ."

Music

25

Dear Readers,

Why do we study music? That's a question that many of you might ask. You think, "I know I like music. I listen to it all the time. So why do I have to understand how it works?"

That's a fair question. And here's one answer that starts with another question.

Have you ever traveled to a place where people speak a different language than you? Maybe they also eat different foods than you are used to, wear different clothing, and listen to different music. Because you are bright and open-minded, you can enjoy this place and its people, even though you don't understand what they are talking about. But if you did learn their language, you would enjoy it and experience it at a completely different and more rewarding level.

Music is much the same. We all love music and, like visiting a new land, we can enjoy it even if we don't understand it all. But if we take the time to learn the language of music, we will experience it and enjoy it at an altogether different and more rewarding level.

Besides that, "Music Rocks!" So who wouldn't want to know as much about it as possible?

Come on! Get on board the Music Express! We've got a lot to learn.

Your friend, John

EXPRESS YOURSELF
Starter Phrase:

"Music rocks because . . ."

26

Dear Readers,

Did you ever have an idea that came into your head that you thought was so great that you didn't want to forget it? Maybe it was a story you wanted to tell or a note you wanted to write to someone. I don't know about you, but for me, if I don't write it down quickly, it often slips right out of my head. A few hours later, I often can't remember what that thought was about! If I do write it down, it helps me remember and allows me to share it with another person or the rest of the world. Wouldn't it be difficult if you couldn't write anything down so that you could remember it later?

Do you ever find yourself walking or running around, or even sitting quietly someplace, and out of nowhere, a tune or melody slips into your head? Maybe it's something that you have heard before and now you are just reminded of it. But maybe it's a brand new idea that nobody in the universe has ever heard except you. Yet there it is, in your head and heart. It might have been triggered by a bubbling brook, the song of a bird, the whiz of traffic, or the cry of a child. Now, there it is floating around from ear to ear, right inside your very full head!

Just like writing down an idea for a story or a note you want to write, being able to write down your musical ideas is a wonderful thing. Being able to write it down will help you remember it later and allow you to share it with your friends, your neighbors or the entire world. What could be more wonderful than sharing your song with the people around you? This is what Mozart, Bach, Beethoven and our other composer friends did all the time. And listen! People are still able to hear their musical messages long after they are gone. You can do it too!

Learning to write music is one of the greatest gifts you can give to yourself and your world. Each of you can do it! You may never get to be as famous as Bach or Beethoven, but if you write down your music so that others can enjoy it, you might be remembered for a long time. And who knows? Just like Stravinsky, you may even get a star in Hollywood some day! Go ahead, be a Mozart! I believe in you!

EXPRESS YOURSELF
Starter Phrase:

Write the words to a song you would like to write music for someday. If you can already write music, write that down too.

Dear Readers,

Yes! It's Music in Our Schools month . . . a time to celebrate all of the magic that music brings to our lives. The word "magic" has a lot of meanings, but when it comes to music, I think it means that it has an extraordinary power to make us feel things like joy, courage, energy and sometimes, even sadness. No hocus-pocus. It's just the magic in the music!

Have you ever watched a movie or a television show with the volume turned off on the TV? It loses a lot, doesn't it? Imagine if there was no music during a chase scene or tear-jerker ending. I guarantee that there would be a lot fewer gasps and tears if there were no music involved. Music makes the difference.

Sometimes when I go to the dentist, she lets me wear a set of earphones so I can listen to my favorite music while she drills away. I get so caught up in the magic of the music, that I hardly feel a thing.

When I go for a run or do some other exercise, I often listen to music to keep my mind off the pain of the experience. The magic in the music helps me go faster, farther, longer.

When I want to relax, I listen to the magic in the music. When I want to forget about something, I let the magic of the music take me away! When I want to get all hyped up, you guessed it! Music is the magic for me!

I hope that during this Music in Our Schools month, you let music be the magic for you, too.

Your friend,
John

EXPRESS YOURSELF
Starter Phrase:

I listen to music when I _____, because _____.

Dear Readers,

One time not too many years ago, I got on an airplane and traveled to Japan to teach music to an elementary school in Tokyo.

Needless to say, I was very excited to meet these young musicians, but I was a little nervous, too. Why was I nervous? Well, you see, I don't speak any Japanese at all. Oh, I can say "hello," "good bye" and even "thank you very much." But, how was that going to help me teach music to a whole school full of Japanese students?

All the way to Japan on the airplane, I got more and more nervous. "This is going to go very poorly," I thought to myself. "I never should have agreed to do this."

When I got off the airplane, my friend met me and we boarded a train for the big city. She told me that there were 600 children waiting to meet me. "Oh no!" I thought. "I have nothing to say to them. This is going to be a disaster!"

We got off the train and walked through the winding streets of Tokyo until we came to the school full of Japanese-speaking readers. By now, I was a nervous wreck! Wouldn't you be, too? But I put on my best face, stood up straight, and walked into the auditorium, ready to meet my fate.

And guess what! As the doors swung open, all 600 Japanese students and their teachers stood up, scooped their hands to the ceiling, and sang the words "The World Sings!"

Then I knew that everything was going to be "Subarashi!" (That's a Japanese word for "wonderful!")

Music is a bridge that brings us together. Those students in Japan knew it. I know it! Now, you know it, too.

Your friend,
John

EXPRESS YOURSELF
Starter Phrase:

Write a story about where music made a difference in your life, or where music was like a bridge between people.

Dear Readers,

Leroy Anderson was an interesting man and a great American Composer. He wrote a lot of different kinds of music, but, the compositions he is most remembered for are the ones where he seems to have heard music playing in some very interesting places—like a typewriter, a jukebox, a clock or even a sleigh. Then he wrote it down.

Do you ever hear music when you listen to something in everyday life? Maybe it's the rhythm of the sound the car makes when it drives over a series of cracks in the highway. Maybe music is in the sound of your feet shuffling along the sidewalk, or a stream running past your window, a motor running or even the wind rustling through the leaves of a tree. I know that sometimes when I go running, the rhythm of my feet and my beating heart give me an idea for a new song. I guess that what Leroy Anderson realized was that there is music all around us and even inside of us, if we only open our ears and our hearts to hear it.

Of all the months, perhaps December contains the most natural music of all. Can you think of some everyday sounds that happen especially in December? How about the clanging of the bell at the Salvation Army collection post? How about jingle bells on a sleigh? To some people, there may even be music in the "ching ching ka-ching" of the cash register after a holiday shopper makes a big purchase. Is there music in the "swoosh swoosh swoosh" of a skier or snowboarder? Okay, none of these sounds might make a complete song or even a very small symphony, but all of them might be the beginning of a work of music, if we listen to their rhythm, their tone or their melody, like Leroy Anderson did with a typewriter.

Defining the difference between music and noise is not easy, but it's kind of nice to know that the world around us is filled with beautiful sounds that may indeed have music inside of them. We just have to listen for it and maybe even sing along. Can you do that? I think you can.

Your friend, John

EXPRESS YOURSELF
Starter Phrase:

The most memorable December day I have had was . . .

30

Dear Readers,

When I was a teenager, I got the wonderful opportunity to play a character named Baby John in a live production of the musical *West Side Story*. It was one of the most amazing musical experiences of my life. Although the musical was about rival gangs in New York City, it was full of exciting music and athletic dancing. I remember working very hard on the dance moves trying my best to get them just right.

During the first scene on opening night, I was supposed to crawl over a high fence on the stage and jump quietly to the ground, as though I was sneaking up on someone. The audience was watching me, but as I climbed over the fence, one of my shoelaces caught in the top of the fence and I fell straight down, head first with a loud thump on the stage. I was not hurt. Needless to say, I **was** mortified, but I jumped back up and continued on as though it was supposed to happen this way. Truthfully, I think only the other cast members knew that it wasn't. Before you knew it, the wonderful music had swept us away and we were all "cool" again.

Little did I know then, that many years later, I would have the privilege of meeting the son of the composer of *West Side Story*, Alexander Bernstein. Leonard Bernstein is his father. I can't begin to tell you how excited I was.

To say that Leonard Bernstein is one of my heroes is an understatement. Here's why. Leonard Bernstein believed that music could change the world. Leonard Bernstein believed that music could bring people together, make people feel connected to one another and treat each other with more kindness and respect. Leonard Bernstein believed that music could make gangs get along and if it could work for gangs, why not families, why not countries, why not the world?

Leonard Bernstein believed that music could make the world we live in better. Me too. That's why he's my hero. And now his son is my friend.

I'm a lucky guy. Let music be a part of your life and together we can change the world!

Your friend, John

EXPRESS YOURSELF
Starter Phrase:

"Music can . . . "

Dear Readers,

I'm sure that you have all heard about the fact that no two snowflakes are exactly alike. Also, no two grains of sand, no two flowers, no two trees, no two feathers, no two people are exactly the same. Guess what? No two voices are exactly the same either! Some of us have high voices, others very low. Some of us have tiny and soft voices; others are big and loud. Some voices sort of wobble when they sing, and others are straight as can be. Some of us sound like we're talking through our noses, while some of our voices are all over the place. In our lifetime, our voices change. They grow with us, just like the rest of our bodies and hopefully, our minds. But no matter how much it changes, your voice will always be unique to you. No one else will sound exactly like you.

Nowhere are different voices more obvious than when we are making music. With all of the different sounds that we make, sometimes it can be quite a challenge to make it sound very good at all, especially when we are all trying to put our voices together. That's why one of the most important parts about making music is listening to the other people with whom you are singing or playing. If you listen to the others around you while you are making your own music, you can adjust it so that the different sounds start to go together. They blend, like the flowers in a bouquet or the colors in a painting, hopefully making something that is satisfying in the end.

The most important thing to remember is that no matter what kind of voice you have, loud or soft, big or little, high or low, nasally or not, **it's yours**. No one can ever take it away from you and if you use it wisely, no one can ever completely drown you out. The trick is to learn to listen. After all, you have two ears and only one mouth. I think that means you should listen twice as much as you talk. Then when you do use your voice, learn to use it well, because it's yours — all yours. And how you use your voice says a lot about who you are. I, for one, think you are all pretty special and when you use your unique voice to make beautiful music, you can make the whole world sing, one by one and all together.

Your friend,
John

EXPRESS YOURSELF
Starter Phrase:

Write a story or a poem that begins with
"I will use my voice to...."

Dear Readers,

People like you are doing the same thing all over the world. In fact, today I'm writing to you from deep in the bush of Africa. Really! I'm on a safari, and when I woke up in my Rondawel (a thatched circular building) this morning, I heard the most amazing natural symphony I have ever heard. Do you know what a symphony is? A symphony is a musical composition. To play a symphony, many instruments and people work together to create something wonderful in a group we call an orchestra.

That's what I heard in the wild this morning – something composed of various elements that, when put together, made a natural orchestra. There were the sounds of the elephants. Their songs are like the brass instruments in the orchestra; when they want to be heard, they can really blare. The lions growl and roar like rolling timpani, or maybe like a fine bass violin. The birds are certainly like the woodwinds; some twitter like a piccolo, while others sing like an oboe or clarinet. Some voice an ostinato pattern over and over and over and over. Do you know what an ostinato is? Do you know what an ostinato is? Do you know what an ostinato is? Ask your teacher.

When I listened to all of those animals making those sounds this morning, it reminded me of the sounds of a rousing orchestra, or for that matter, a beautiful choir. Each instrument that plays or voice that sings is unique and wonderful all by itself. But when you put them all together, they make something completely new — something none of them can do all by themselves. We need all of the instruments doing their part to make the music sound just right. In the same way, we need each of you to do your very best in school all year long, so that together, we can make something wonderful and exciting happen — just like the animals in the jungle or the fantastic instruments of the orchestra.

Your friend,
John

EXPRESS YOURSELF
Starter Phrase:

If I were a musical instrument, I would be a
_____, and here is why...

Dear Readers,

I can only remember bits and pieces of most of the dances I have learned in my life, but I can remember almost all of the very first song and dance I ever learned and performed with my choir when I was growing up in a little town in Wisconsin. The song was Irving Berlin's classic "Alexander's Ragtime Band."

The words began, "Come on and hear! Come on and hear Alexander's Ragtime Band!" Looking at those lyrics, you can probably imagine what the dance moves were. My choir and I wore bright red vests. We marched and did the old-fashioned dance called the Charleston. We pretended to play musical instruments like a real brass band and wore ice cream hats we called skimmers. It was my first taste of show business and I fell in love with it!

Believe me when I tell you that it wasn't the wonderful choreography that made our performance memorable. Even though we were very proud of ourselves, it was clear that the reason people were clapping along was because "Alexander's Ragtime Band" is one of the catchiest songs ever written. That should come as no surprise because Irving Berlin was perhaps America's greatest songwriter ever. Period!

Have you ever heard the song "White Christmas?" "White Christmas" was written by Irving Berlin. How about "God Bless America?" You guessed it—the one and only Irving Berlin.

"Alexander's Ragtime Band" is more than 100 years old. To me, great songs never go out of style, and a hundred years from now, I bet people will still be singing, "Come on and hear! Come on and hear Alexander's Ragtime Band." After today, you are all a part of that great tradition, too. Thanks, Mr. Berlin, for letting us come along and join your singing band!

EXPRESS YOURSELF
Starter Phrase:

My favorite tradition is . . .

34

Dear Readers,

What do you hear when you step outside in the morning? Maybe you hear birds singing, or bees and mosquitoes buzzing around your ears. Maybe you live in the city and hear the sound of cars, trucks and motorcycles revving their engines, or trains rumbling along their tracks. Maybe you hear a baby crying in the house next door or, if you live by an ocean, the surf crashing against the shoreline time after time.

What do you hear when you go out of the classroom during the school day? Do you hear basketballs bouncing or soccer balls being kicked in the gymnasium? Maybe you hear the cooks in the cafeteria cleaning pots and pans or stirring up something with a wooden spoon. Maybe you hear the shuffle of other students' feet along the hallway, the closing of locker doors or the voices of teachers echoing in the halls.

What do you hear when you are absolutely quiet and all by yourself? Do you hear your heart beating, your breath going in and out, your knuckles cracking, your toes tapping?

These are all the sounds of life.

What we do when we make music is that we take the sounds of life and turn them into the *song* of life. Music is organized. It has form. It has melody. It has rhythm and harmony, tone and color. This year we are going to learn how to listen more closely to the sounds of life all around us and learn how to organize all that noise into something very beautiful – something we call music. What could be more exciting than that? You, your teacher and I will make music together, because I am...

EXPRESS YOURSELF
Starter Phrase:

Write a poem, a song or a story entitled
"The Song of Life."

Dear Readers,

Did you ever notice how much music goes on at most sporting events? I do ... especially at a baseball game.

Like right from the very beginning when we all stand and sing "The Star Spangled Banner." I used to get so embarrassed when I was a kid because my Dad would always sing our national anthem at the top of his lungs. I couldn't wait for it to be over. Guess what? Now that I'm an adult, I do exactly the same thing! I guess when you get older, you realize how lucky we are to live in such a wonderful country as America. When I see all of the players put their caps over their hearts, the umpires and coaches standing at attention and the fans quietly facing the flag, I realize that this country is something of which to be proud. It makes me want to sing! Go on. I dare you!

Then there's that time in the seventh inning where everybody stops, stretches and sings "Take Me Out to the Ball Game." I'm always surprised that even people who hardly ever sing outside of the shower, bellow away when they link elbows and sing this song. Even if some of them could use a few more voice lessons, I think it's great!

I like when the organ in the big stadium gets everyone clapping along, or when they play "da da da da da da!" and everyone yells "CHARGE!!" Sometimes they play the chorus from "Aye Japonicas Aye Aye" and everyone claps just when they are supposed to, or they play "WE WILL, WE WILL ROCK YOU" and everybody gets into it and sings along. There's music in the voices of the popcorn sellers or the peanut vendors, maybe even in the shuffling of the feet of fans.

Baseball – America's musical pastime!

I like it. I like it a lot!

Let's play ball!

Your friend, John

EXPRESS YOURSELF
Starter Phrase:

"My favorite pastime is _____ and here is why."

Dear Readers,

My friend Audrey Snyder has written us a beautiful, brand new song called "My Song." Maybe you have already learned it. It starts out . . .

My song comes from deep inside of me.
My song is my own melody.
When I am happy or even when I'm blue,
I let my song come through.

I love it. I believe that everybody has a song inside that is uniquely . . . you. For some of us, our song might be playing sports, or playing a musical instrument. For others, your song might be math or working with computers, growing a garden, or writing an exciting story. Like snowflakes and flowers, no two songs are exactly alike. Thank goodness! Wouldn't it be boring if everybody always sang the same song, or even got excited or good at the very same things?

What makes the world so colorful, interesting and even harmonious is that we all are different. We all look different. We are all interested in different things. We are all good at different things. We even each sing a different song.

So, have you ever thought about your song? Don't worry, you don't have to name it and you don't have to sing just one song. There might be lots of "notes" inside of you that make you sing. You might be someone who likes sports a little, computer games a lot, and music like it's the most important thing in the world; or you might be a person who mostly likes to cook, jump rope or watch movies. Whatever is the combination of interests and talents that make you sing, that's what makes your song. And you know what? It's beautiful!

I hope that each and every one of you agree that happiness is . . . exploring the song that is inside you and when you find it . . . sing it!

EXPRESS YOURSELF
Starter Phrase:

This is My Song ...

Holidays and Happenings

37

Dear Readers,

Happy New Year!

What a wonderful year this is going to be! The days will soon begin to lengthen as a sure sign of spring. The Super Bowl is just around the corner — Valentine's Day, too.

The start of a New Year is always a good time to think about new beginnings. It's a time to change bad habits and consider the exciting things you want to do in the next twelve months and beyond. It's sort of like taking a shower. You spray off the old dirt of yesteryear, dry yourself off and start all over again, all clean and refreshed.

It doesn't matter too much how things have been going up to this point. When the New Year bell rings and we all sing "Auld Lang Syne," we each have an opportunity to turn over a new leaf and change the things that feel wrong in our lives. Maybe you think that you haven't been nice enough to your parents, brothers and sisters, teachers or even your friends. Maybe you aren't happy about your study habits, your eating habits or your exercise routine. Well...

Today is a chance for a new beginning for you, for me, for everybody. It doesn't have to happen on January 1st. It can be any day that you decide you want things to be different. With the dawn of a new year, anything is possible. As it says "Good Morning," I feel sure that for all of us, a new beginning starts today.

Your friend,
John

EXPRESS YOURSELF

Starter Phrase:

This year, I'm going to make a new beginning by . . .

38

Dear Readers,

Happy New Year! It looks like it is going to be a very exciting one!

Did you ever find yourself waiting in line and it seems to take forever to get your turn? It might be waiting in a lunch line with your hungry stomach growling, or perhaps when you are waiting to buy tickets for a movie theater, or waiting your turn to play a classroom instrument, or waiting to be chosen to answer a question or to be picked for a team. Sometimes the waiting can seem to take forever. You might see a lot of good things happening to someone that you know. Maybe it's an older brother or sister or one of your friends. They seem to get to do things you never get to do. You wonder "when will it be my time?"

In the olden days, children in schools would write their lessons on small chalkboards made out of slate. They used chalk so that the slate could be wiped clean after each lesson and they could start fresh. A new year is like starting with a "clean slate." You decide what to write on it.

This is your time! You can choose how you want to move forward in this new year. You, each of you, is at the front of a line of one. What will you decide to do with this gift of time? I hope that you will decide to move forward with real enthusiasm in all aspects of your life. At school, at home, on the playground or wherever you find yourself, I hope you will remind yourself it's finally your turn. You have a clean slate and you can decide how you want to fill it.

There will be lots of people to help you along the way, especially your teachers. They want to help you make the most of your clean slate, but in the end, it's up to you. This is your time!

Go for it.

Your friend,
John

EXPRESS YOURSELF

Starter Phrase:

Write a poem or a story with the title A Brand New Day!

39

Dear Readers,

I wanted to tell you about a good friend of mine. Her name is Helen Freeman. She teaches music to children in Arizona. She has 10 children of her own. She also takes care of lots of others, including me sometimes!

Not very long ago, Helen Freeman's house burned right to the ground. Luckily, nobody was hurt, but Helen and her family lost everything they owned. I think that they were very sad when they first thought about all of the pictures they lost. But in another way, Helen told me that it was "kind of nice to be able to start life all over again without a bunch of things to weigh us down."

I thought a lot about what Helen said. You know what? I think she's right!

Sometimes it seems like we all worry too much about having a lot of nice things. We like to have new clothes to wear, even when we have older ones that are just fine. We feel like we need to have the newest video game, the very best skateboard, another pair of shoes.

During Black History month, I often think about those African Americans who worked so hard to make our country better – people like George Washington Carver, Booker T. Washington, Martin Luther King, Harriet Tubman. I don't think anyone of them felt like they needed a lot of things to make their life complete. They just needed a chance.

From now on, I'm going to do my best to quit looking for new things and start looking for new chances to make the world better.

How about you?

EXPRESS YOURSELF
Starter Phrase:

Whatever day of the year it is, my New Year's resolution is …

40

Dear Readers,

This is the time of year when Americans take time to give thanks. In fact, we take a day or two off to do exactly that. Well, we eat too much and watch a little football too. But mostly we pause to give thanks for the wonderful lives we can lead here in the country we know as, the United States of America.

As Americans, we have so much for which to be thankful. What are you thankful for this year? Here's a small part of my very long list.

I'm thankful that I live in a country that believes that learning is very important. So, every single American child has a school to go to because Americans know that a citizen with a good education will be a better American.

I'm thankful that I live in a country where every person has a place in the choir. It doesn't matter your race or color, language or creed, in America, you belong.

Speaking of choirs, I'm thankful for students like you who keep an open mind to new ideas. Did you ever hear a song for the first time and think "Oh, I don't like that"? But the more times you listen to it, or maybe even learn the notes, rhythms and words, it kind of grows on you. Pretty soon you actually kind of like it. I'm thankful for students who like to try new things.

Likewise, I'm thankful for students like you who keep an open mind and heart when meeting new people. Just like that song you heard once and thought you didn't like, the more you learned about it, the more you liked it. When you meet someone new for the first time, it's best to not decide that you don't like them. It's better to give them a chance, or a thousand chances. Eventually, you might see how lucky you are to have met that special person.

Wouldn't it be a boring country if everybody in it were exactly alike? I give thanks to you America that you stand for the fact that different is okay. In fact, it may be the very thing that makes the United States of America great!

Your friend,
John

EXPRESS YOURSELF
Starter Phrase:

Write a story that begins like this:
"I was feeling very out of place...
and ends like this "For that I am very thankful!"

Dear Readers,

In the autumn, we celebrate two different holidays that are both about saying "Thank you." On November 11th, we celebrate the holiday known as Veterans Day. On Veterans Day, we take time out of our schedules to think about the fine men and women who have served our country in our military. These are people who have taken time out of their lives and away from their families to make sure that people all over the world can live in peace. What a wonderful goal! What a splendid dream!

Later in November, we celebrate Thanksgiving Day. On this day, we give thanks for everything good in our lives — our friends, our families, our teachers, our schools, the food we eat, the air we breath, the dreams we have — everything! It's nice to think about how the two holidays of November fit so well together. On one day, we think of our veterans and the dreams they protect; on the other day we give thanks for everything else.

What are you thankful for this November? I know I'm thankful that I live in a country where everyone is encouraged to dream and then to wake up and follow those dreams. I'm also thankful that young people all over the world are learning about music and about the important role that music plays in our lives. Wouldn't it be hard to follow your dreams if you didn't have music to help you along? Like a good movie, most of my dreams come with their own soundtrack. Sometimes it's a race scene. Sometimes it's light and floating. But music is always there to make every dream more fantastic.

This November, I'm thankful for veterans, for children who love music, and, without a doubt, for colorful dreams.

EXPRESS YOURSELF
Starter Phrase:

This year I am especially thankful for _____, and here is why ...

42

Dear Readers,

Let's celebrate music! For when you celebrate music, you celebrate life!

It is true that the most important moments in our lives are often best remembered by the music that accompanied them. Do you remember your last birthday? Everybody sang "Happy Birthday to You" and maybe gave you a spanking or two. That singing of a song on your birthday happens to children all over the world. It's one of the ways we celebrate life with music. (I'm not sure if they do the spanking part all over the world or not!)

At the beginning of a sporting event, the entire crowd stands and sings our National Anthem. That happens all over the world, too. Remember when you watched the medal ceremonies from the Olympics? Through the smiles and tears, the champions basked in their success, listening to and singing the music of their homeland. Next time you are at a sporting event or anywhere where our National Anthem is sung, I hope that you will stand and sing with your whole heart. It's another one of the ways in which we use music to celebrate life.

At baseball games, people link arms and sing "Take Me Out to the Ballgame!" At graduation ceremonies, the band plays "Pomp and Circumstance" as the graduates proudly process down the aisles, and someone sings "Climb Every Mountain" as they exit to take on the world. At weddings, Moms and Dads and ex-boyfriends cry when someone sings "The Rose" right before the couple kisses. On the Fourth of July, cannons fire as orchestras play "The 1812 Overture" while fireworks light up the sky.

Music is everywhere, everyday of our lives. With a little imagination, some will say you can even hear music in the sound of a brook bubbling over the rocks, in the wind as it whistles through the trees, or even in the traffic as it snarls a busy street. In every case, music makes it beautiful!

So come on, let's celebrate music! For when you celebrate music, you celebrate life!

Your
friend,
John

EXPRESS YOURSELF
Starter Phrase:

"The best way to celebrate life is......

Dear Readers,

On the eleventh hour, (that would be eleven in the morning), on the eleventh day of the eleventh month, (that would be November) in the year of 1919, what has become to be known as World War One or The War to End All Wars came to an end. The powers-that-be signed a treaty at the Palace of Versailles in France and it was, at last, a done deal.

Our President at the time was Woodrow Wilson and he proclaimed that November 11 would from that day forward be called Armistice Day. An armistice is when opposing sides come together and make a truce for peace. In President Wilson's words, it "will be a day filled with solemn pride in the heroism of those who died in the country's service..."

Unfortunately, World War One was not the War to End All Wars and our country has had many more heroes to honor from conflicts all over the world, many of whom are even serving today. Some of them you might even know.

So, since 1954 Armistice Day has been known instead as Veterans Day. On this very special day, we stop as Americans and think about all of the fine men and women, brothers and sisters, sons and daughters, moms and dads, uncles, aunts, grandparents and friends who have given so much of themselves to make certain we can live free in this proud and beautiful nation.

We thank them by working our hardest to do our best everyday in school. We thank them by showing good sportsmanship on the playground and good citizenship all around town. We try to be heroes in our own way by doing right by each other and in doing so, make ourselves worthy of our veterans' heroism.

Once a year, it is *a time to remember,* and, to all the veterans we know and even those we don't know, say "Thank you! I will try with my whole heart to reflect your heroism in my life every single day." Now, it is November and once again, it is that time to remember. Lest we forget . . .

EXPRESS YOURSELF
Starter Phrase:

Today I will write about a hero in my life.
Their name is . . .

Dear Readers,

For many people, December is a time of snow and icicles, frozen ponds and sleigh rides. However, for people who live in other parts of the world, the experience is a much different one. For people who live in places like Florida, or Texas, Tahiti, or Timbuktu, December memories include days spent on a sunny beach wearing sandals and suntan lotion. Instead of decorating fir trees or spruce, these people might hang lights from a palm tree or a banana plant. Instead of skiing down a snow-covered slope, people who live in the tropics might spend the afternoon surfing or boogie boarding in the sun.

It must feel kind of strange for people who live in warm winter climates to always be hearing songs about jingling bells ringing from a sleigh, skaters waltzing, frosted window panes, and dancing snowmen. In the same way, it can sometimes be hard for people who live in the snow to imagine a Christmas Day or New Year's Eve without having to wear layers of warm clothes and gulping down hot chocolate to try to stay warm.

Even though it is true that some parts of the holiday experience are very different for people around the world, one thing is clear as a December night. For those that truly celebrate the winter holidays of Christmas, Kwanzaa, Hanukkah or Ramadan, warm or cold, sunning or shivering, we all share the same sweet wish for peace on Earth and good will toward all. That's something to celebrate!

I hope that your December holidays are wonderful, whether you are singing in the snow or dancing in the sun!

EXPRESS YOURSELF
Starter Phrase:

"This winter, I want to . . . "

Dear Readers,

What is the most joyful noise you have ever heard? Is it when the sports announcer shouts, "Gooooooaaaaaal"? Is it when a baby laughs, or when a screaming baby stops screaming and starts to giggle? Is it when your teacher says, "Time for recess"? Is it when your friends are all laughing together or when you hear bells ringing, birds singing, trumpets blaring or cats purring?

All over the world, December is a time when people talk a lot about **joy**. They sing words like "Joy to the world" and "Love and joy come to you, and to you a wassail too." Everywhere you go, you can hear and feel the joy of this season as we close out one year and head into another.

I have a challenge for all of you this December. I challenge you to go out and try especially hard to spread your joy. Do something extra kind for somebody and see if you can recognize when your action brings joy to that person. Say something nice to somebody you've never complimented before. Do a favor for someone who least expects it. Write a thank-you note to someone important in your life. Think of at least three ways that you can share your joy this December, and I promise it will come back to you ten times over.

There is an old saying that goes, "It is better to give than to receive." This December, I challenge you to try this saying out and see if it is true. I think you will find that it is, especially if what you give is sincere and filled with genuine joy.

Do you want to know what sound brings me joy? It's the sound of people like you making music and spreading their joy through their music.

Go ahead. This December, make my day and let's work together to make a joyful noise!

EXPRESS YOURSELF
Starter Phrase:

I can spread joy by . . .

Dear Readers,

Did you know that when Irving Berlin was writing the famous song "White Christmas," he was sitting by a swimming pool in very sunny Phoenix, Arizona? He found himself dreaming of the snowy and cold winters that he remembered from his earlier days in New York City.

I think the holiday season is a good one in which to day or night dream. I'm wondering what all of you are dreaming about these days.

I'm dreaming that all young people 'round the world will continue to love music as much as I do. I'm dreaming that those same young people will learn to value the wonderful role that music plays in their lives. I'm dreaming that they will learn to be good listeners of music, so that they can tell the difference between music that brings us down or lifts us up. I'm dreaming that they will learn to enjoy memorizing songs and learning dances and movements that go along with some of them, and that they will share their music with other people in their lives. I'm dreaming that they realize that when you share your time and talent with others, you are giving the greatest gift you have to offer. It's rather easy to go to a store and buy a present for someone, but when you take the time to learn and perform on a musical instrument, go caroling to people who need some holiday cheer, or do something else that's just plain nice, you have given perhaps the finest present of all — a part of yourself.

This December, I'm dreaming that everyone will be more kind to each other. I'm dreaming that we will always look for the good in our neighbors and friends. I'm dreaming that we will easily recognize the beautiful song that is in everyone, and that we will encourage them to sing it.

Won't you help make my December dream come true? I knew you would.

EXPRESS YOURSELF
Starter Phrase:

This December, I'm dreaming . . .

Dear Readers,

What does the word "miracle" mean to you?

In my dictionary, the word "miracle" is defined as "an event or action that is totally amazing, extraordinary, or unexpected." In another definition, a miracle is "an event that appears to be contrary to the laws of nature."

A small child was lost in the cold winter woods. As the blizzard grows worse and her predicament more desperate, it seems that a terrible tragedy might well occur. Instead, a miracle happens. Animals of the forest, some who are the natural enemy of another, come together to protect the small child from the elements. Together they keep her warm and in the morning, lead her back to safety. It's amazing! It's extraordinary! It's unexpected! It's a miracle!

From my point of view, amazing things seem to happen every single day. The moon goes down, pulling the tides of the ocean along with it. The sun comes up, lighting and warming the world. Plants grow and flowers bloom. Hearts beat, lungs fill with air, birds sing, children too. But these amazing things have happened so many times that by now we have all come to expect them. To be a "miracle," it cannot be ordinary. It must be "amazing" and "unexpected."

In December, most people on Earth celebrate happenings so rare and astounding that they can be nothing other than miracles. Most of these miracles are events that happened a long time ago, a baby born in a manger or oil enough for a night that instead, burned for eight. There are others, too. Miracles have happened before, but there is always the possibility that a miracle will happen, today as well. A lion may lie down with a lamb. A hungry child who has never giggled, may smile at the kindness of a stranger. The whole world may unexpectedly decide that it is time to sing the same harmonious song.

A great American author named Willa Cather once wrote, "Where there is great love, there will always be miracles." Aha! So that's the key ingredient for miracles. Love! Love in the light of a luminario. Love in a stable near Bethlehem. Love beneath a tree in the cold woods. December is a time of amazing, extraordinary and often unexpected love. December is a time for miracles.

Watch for them.

Your friend,
John

EXPRESS YOURSELF
Starter Phrase:

A miracle happened when...

Dear Readers,

It's an exciting time of year, isn't it? All of the important winter holidays are almost here. It's hard not to get excited about the parties, the decorations, the songs and the gifts that come our way during this special time of the year. People all over the world are celebrating in their very own way and in their very own language.

There is a phrase that I first learned in Germany many years ago. It goes like this,

"Freudenkinder mögen Gäste. Zeigen Sie ihnen den Weg."

Try to say it. It has a nice sound.

"Freudenkinder mögen Gäste. Zeigen Sie ihnen den Weg."

It means, "Treat children as guests. Show them the way." It's a nice thought, isn't it?

It's true that part of what it means to be a grownup is to show children the way through life. It's the grownup's job to teach you right from wrong, show you how to do things and how to be safe. It's an adult's job to teach you how to learn and even how to celebrate. Taking the time to "show children the way" is about the best gift that an adult can give to a child, in December or any time of the year.

Of course, when you receive a gift from someone, there is something very important that a guest should do in return, isn't there?

That's right! You say, "Thank you," or "Vielen Dank," if you're in Germany. I hope you remember to say "thank you" for all of the wonderful gifts that come your way this holiday season. It's what thoughtful guests always do.

Happy Holidays!

Your friend,
John

EXPRESS YOURSELF
Starter Phrase:

"I hope for . . ."

(49)

Dear Readers,

Can you remember the first day of school this year? You were probably pretty excited to get back together with your old friends or, if this is a new school for you, excited to make some new ones.

You were maybe a little bit nervous, too. It can be pretty frightening to start an adventure like a new school year. You wonder if you will fit in. You wonder if you will be able to keep up. You wonder if you'll make it to the end of the year.

Well, guess what? The end of the school year for most of you is just around the corner. You made it! And I feel pretty sure that you did a good job along the way.

It probably seems like a long time ago that you started this grade level. Can you name a few things that you know now that you didn't know when you started this year? Of course, you can. Although you are the same person you were when you started this grade, you have changed. You may have gotten taller. You may be able to do things, read things and figure things out that you couldn't do just a few months ago. You've come a long way.

So I just wanted to say congratulations to each and every one of you! You've got a lot to look forward to, and all of your teachers – myself included – are really rooting for you.

Yes, you've changed, and just look how far you've come!

Your friend,
John

EXPRESS YOURSELF
Starter Phrase:

"Here is a list of some of the best things I've learned so far this year..."

50

Dear Readers,

I don't know about you, but I have a huge family – nine brothers and sisters, twenty-four nieces and nephews, and now a grandnephew and two grandnieces. The newest one was just born. Her name is Stella, and judging by her voice, I think she's going to be a great Music Express kid herself someday, just like you!

One of my favorite events each year is when we get together for a big family reunion. We actually do it pretty often considering we live quite far apart. We pack up the kids, cats, dogs and everything else and find almost any excuse to get together. When we do, it's always a lot of fun, and there is always music involved.

Getting together for a family reunion is much like gathering a group of instrumentalists together to form a band or a symphony. It is also a lot like gathering a group of singers to make a choir. Often, everybody who gathers plays something that sounds different from the person behind or in front of them. In a chorus, certainly no two voices sound exactly alike. But when you put them all together and they all try their very best to blend their sounds, it can be as beautiful and harmonious as, well, a great big family!

Whether you come from a big family or not, one thing is for sure: in music you will always have lots of brothers and sisters. There will always be a place for you, and with those brothers and sisters, together you can make harmony happen — like a symphony, like a choir, like a family!

Your friend,
John

EXPRESS YOURSELF
Starter Phrase:

I want to bring people together
a.) to . . .
b.) with . . .
c.) like . . .
d.) on . . .
e.) at . . .

Choose a preposition from the list above and create your paragraph.

About the Writer:
John Jacobson

In October of 2001 President George Bush named John Jacobson a Point of Light award winner for his "dedication to providing young people involved in the arts opportunities to combine music, charitable giving and community service." John is the founder and volunteer president of America Sings! Inc., a non-profit organization that encourages young performers to use their time and talents for community service. With a bachelor's degree in Music Education from the University of Wisconsin-Madison and a Master's Degree in Liberal Studies from Georgetown University, John is recognized internationally as a creative and motivating speaker for teachers and students involved in choral music education. He is the author and composer of many musicals and choral works that have been performed by millions of children worldwide, as well as educational videos and tapes that have helped music educators excel in their individual teaching arenas, all published exclusively by Hal Leonard Corporation. John has staged hundreds of huge music festival ensembles in his association with Walt Disney Productions and directed productions featuring thousands of young singers including NBC's national broadcast of the Macy's Thanksgiving Day Parade, presidential inaugurations and more. John stars in children's musical and exercise videotapes, including the series *Jjump!,* A Fitness Program for Children and is the Senior Contributing Writer for John Jacobson's *Music Express*, an educational magazine for young children published by Hal Leonard Corporation. Most recently, John has become a YouTube sensation and is known by millions as the "Double Dream Hands Guy!"